OLD WOMAN COMES OUT OF HER CAVE

Old Woman Comes Out Of Her Cave

by

Mildred Tremblay

OOLICHAN BOOKS
LANTZVILLE, BRITISH COLUMBIA, CANADA
2001

Canadian Cataloguing in Publication Data

Tremblay, Mildred, 1925
    Old woman comes out of her cave

    Poems
    ISBN 0-88982-190-9

    I. Title.
PS8589.R455042 2001   C811'.54   C2001-910721-8
PR9199.3.T649O42 2001

We gratefully acknowledge the support of the Canada Council for the Arts for our publishing program.

THE CANADA COUNCIL | LE CONSEIL DES ARTS
FOR THE ARTS | DU CANADA
SINCE 1957 | DEPUIS 1957

Grateful acknowledgement is also made to the BC Ministry of Tourism, Small Business and Culture for their financial support.

BRITISH
COLUMBIA
ARTS COUNCIL
Supported by the Province of British Columbia

We acknowledge the financial support of the Government of Canada through the Book Publishing Industry Development Program for our publishing activities.

Canada

Published by
Oolichan Books
P.O. Box 10, Lantzville
British Columbia, Canada
V0R 2H0

Printed in Canada

For Suzanne, Leila, Anita, Lorraine,
Joan, Mia and Lance

Acknowledgements

I would like to thank the Nanaimo Women's Writers'
Group for the warmth of their support and for the
magic that happens every time we meet; Winona
Baker, Margo Button and Leanne McIntosh for their
invaluable help and for their loving presence in my
life; my husband and spiritual partner, Ross, who is
always available to listen and who offered many
helpful comments; Patricia Young for her boundless
generosity in sharing her editing skills; and my
publisher, Ron Smith, for his genuine interest in and
support of my work over many years.

Some of the poems in this book were awarded prizes
by the League of Canadian Poets, the Arc National
Poetry Magazine and the Leacock Humour Competi-
tion.

I gratefully acknowledge the financial assistance
received from the Canada Council to complete this
manuscript.

Contents

First Dwelling Place

Astonishing Creations / 13
When My Mother Created The World / 16
Family Ranking / 17
One Potato Two / 18
God's Story / 20
Big Meow / 22
God And Pooch / 24
Children / 26
Winter In Kenora / 27
Boiled Carrots / 29
Blueberry Country / 31
Holiday At Grandma's / 32
The Neighbour's Son / 33
Skinny Bird / 34
Heaven And Hell / 35
Our Lady / 36
My Father Teaches Me About Men / 37
The Bath / 39

Breasts & Bellies

Somewhere A God Laughs / 43
Feeling Fine, Saving Money / 44
Without Warning, My Mother / 45
Breasts And Bellies / 46
Mothers / 48
Meningitis / 50
Drumming Up The Dead / 51
Water / 53
Sudden Death / 54
Rapture Poured In
Where My Mother Had Been / 55
The Midwife / 57
True Love / 58
Marilyn Monroe At The Morgue / 59
The Tolstoys / 60
The Cookie Cutter / 61
Passing Jupiter / 63
Regina Vagina / 64
The Pope Dreams About Women / 66
She No Longer Goes To Church / 67
Quoting Popeye / 68
How The Pope Likes His Women / 70
God Flees The Palace / 71
Blood Fathers / 72
How Does One Dress In Heaven / 73
The Return Of The Mammoth / 77
Once There Were Tigers / 79
Planet Earth / 80
Back On The Longing Train / 81
Stigmata / 82
The Morning Holds Me In Its Arms / 83
God Is Everything / 84
Kubler-Ross And The Cranefly / 85
Post Modern Funerals / 87

Old Woman / 89

Loose Woman / 91
Old Woman Speaks / 93
Codeine And Roses / 94
The Secret / 96
Tryst / 98
A Young Husband / 100
Hound And Old Woman Give Warning / 101
Where Does The Radiance Go / 103
Old Woman Comes Out Of Her Cave And Puts
The World In Order / 104

First Dwelling Place

. . . bounded by the church with its ready
made consolations; clean and disenchanted
and shut as a post office on Sunday.

ɔ. Rainer Maria Rilke

ASTONISHING CREATIONS

In her bedroom Mamma and I
dress for shopping in town.
Her unveiled body is a bounty
of spilled breasts and belly.
Holding her up
are blue legs with bumps.
She is not ashamed
of this astonishing creation;
I can look as much as I please.

I poke the wrinkled warm belly.
I am five and already I've forgotten
this first dwelling place,
growing myself, piece by piece
in the dark, beside the blood rivers:
arm buds, brain stem, heart chambers.
My own pearl-sized uterus,
my own tiny baskets of eggs.

Naked, Mamma opens a round blue box,
dips a puff into Evening in Paris,
a Christmas present
bought for a quarter at Woolworth's.
Powder flies like pollen
into creases and undersides
both Mamma's and mine.

Next, her corset a strait jacket
of whalebone and shoelaces.
With pushes and squeezes,
        she hauls herself in;
her breasts lift above,
with the huge blissful nipples
my tongue still remembers.

I wear a white dress with a sash.
She wears a dark suit made to measure
at Tip Top. In the small cluttered shop
she stands still to be measured,
her arms held out like a ruffled duck
while a short bald man who eats pins,
chastely circles her bust and hips
with his long ocher tape.

This suit will see her through
church suppers, bazaars and
prideful meetings of Canadian Daughters.
When it frays, the same little circling
Tip Top man will make another. Same style,
perhaps a slight variation
in fleck or pleat.

In one of these suits, she will lie
in her coffin, her hands
folded obediently
just below the navy blue lapels.
I will be twenty years old;
my breasts large nippled like hers,
my stomach flat as a field but
my future children
already gathering
in impatient clouds around me.

WHEN MY MOTHER CREATED THE WORLD

When my mother created the world
she filled my mouth with suckle
and spurt of warm milk.
She created her face, placed it
above mine. I couldn't stop staring,
her lips flying and flopping,

words drifting down.
mama the lips said *dada*
num num. One day my mother

said *you,* said *me*
drawing me out of paradise

towards the word
loneliness.

FAMILY RANKING

I came in sixth
a risky business
but it was that or nothing

still I reigned secure
Queen of the Crib
until the Usurper arrived

toppled at three
I went on with my life
murder in my heart

ONE POTATO TWO

When I look at my body,
its knobs and foliage,
sinkholes and scars,
furrows of flesh,
I reflect that
going back
to the far mists of Ireland,
to my O'Reilly
and Dolan and Kennedy forerunners,
to Queen Maeve herself
I am

mostly potatoes.

The first solid food
spooned
into my baby bird mouth

was potatoes.

Twice a day on the table
my mother
slapped down
great heaping bowls
of fluffy white clouds
laced with butter and salt.

In Heaven the Holy Family
eats nothing but potatoes.

Sacred Potatoes

washed clean
in the tears of Christ,
cooked to immaculate perfection
by Mary.

In the kitchens of Purgatory,
semi-devils
burn the potatoes
on purpose.

Hell is worse. Hell is
no potatoes at all.

GOD'S STORY

Who made you? God made me. Why did God make
you? God made me to adore, love and envy his Penis.
(Catechism: Book One)

Inside the delivery room, in the belly of the Goddess,
the universe lay in fetal position, hiccupping, sucking
its thumbs, its trillions of faces wrinkled with fright
at the prospect of leaving Mother.

Outside the delivery room, God waited.

From time to time he heard shrieks and gargantuan
groans, followed by laughter and love cries. Ahhh!
Ahhh! The door never opened and no one came out
to speak to him.

Then a shout from the midwife: Brace yourself,
Mother, a galactic cluster is presenting ass first!

God put his eye to the keyhole. The Goddess reclined
in a birth chair, her vagina stretched to the four
corners as she bore down on Cassiopeia.

Awestruck, God reflected for the first time that he was
missing a part. Placing his head between his knees,
he swung his testaments, both old and new, out of
the way, stared at his anus.

Won't do! he said.

Next his navel, his nostrils, and his ears were carefully

probed. Looking down, he happened to spy the eye at the end of his penis. For a moment, alone in the hall, he hesitated, deep in thought, pulling hairs from his beard.

Then he flung open the door, strode into the delivery room. With a supreme sweep of his hand, he laid claim to all of creation.

From this Wondrous Gate, it has sprang! he said to the disbelieving nurses, holding out his penis, and pointing to the pinhole. All of it. That's my story, and by thunder and lightning, I'm sticking to it!

BIG MEOW

Who made you?
Meow made me.

Catechism. (Book One)

In the beginning there was only Big Meow. She sat in
a window, a most exquisite Meow, looking out at
zero. Boring, even for Meow. Let there be something,
She said. And out of nothing, a glittering fish leapt
with a dry splash. Fish is here! Meow exclaimed
stretching Her mouth in a yowl of self praise, display-
ing teeth prettier than polished white pebbles on a
pink petal.

Meanwhile the fish died, having no element. Meow
blinked Her drugged amber eyes, pondered. Ah, Fish
must have something around them! Something below
them and above them. And She thought of a wet
thing full to the top and wrinkled.

Up rose the sea out of zero, slopping and spilling.

Meow jumped down from the window, landing
lightly on paws stuffed with powder puffs. Stepping
outside, She retrieved the dead fish and ate it. As She
chewed on the savory head, She squinted her eyes
almost shut and smiled down into Her neck fur,
wrapped in a rapture. Now for a paw bath, She said,
working up some spit. After that: the ten thousand
things.

So Meow begin to create: Cat naps and cat nip, full moons, fences, and shadows. Hands to ladle out cat chow.

And on the seventh day Meow created Tom. Tom She created so that She might sit on the road and look the other way as if he didn't exist.

GOD AND POOCH

1

In their black high-top shoes, the nuns
stepped darkly into my five-year old mind,
and installed their heavy-faced Gods.
Easter Island megaliths, with a gaze
that seared over playgrounds
towards heaven and hell.

I had no choice
but to befriend them.

Up reared the Bleeding God,
murdered afresh every hour
by my sins. His lily-pure Mother
was a Go-Between Queen
but the one to watch out for
was the Big One
centre stage, with the Eye.
This God they lashed to my back
with a hangman's knot.
He settled there like a hump
and from that moment on
I was followed and watched.

2

Call him Father, Sister said.
You must love him,
this invisible Man, above any other.
What he most likes to hear
is how sorry you are. You
little thief, liar, misser of Mass,
eater of meat on Fridays, you
little clitoris addict.

I understood love very well.
I loved Pooch, my brown and white dog.
Next I loved Sox, the neighbor's dog.
Truth was, I loved any sort of dog,
slobbering or clean.
All it took was a tailwag.

But I didn't love God.

And he knew it.

CHILDREN

Little mothers
pushing prams
swivel
their bottoms
totter
down sidewalks
on borrowed high heels

battered dolls
stare from blankets
bonnets
torn and crooked

Inside forts
little fathers
whittle slingshots
tally up
murdered birds
snicker
over fart
& pecker jokes
ponder
ways to kidnap
& to screw
the little mothers.

WINTER IN KENORA

In Kenora the old people
choose January to die
when the ground resists being opened.
The child believes there are bodies
stacked like frozen fish in the cemetery toolshed
waiting for the cold snap to end.
Her father affirms he has heard
from the shed the sound of teeth chattering.

In the evening after supper
the child helps her father
stack jackpine. The clumsy chunks
are carried into the cellar
laid row upon yellow row.
A glance of approval from the father
and the child loads extra sticks,
her arms almost breaking.
Joy makes her silly; she loves

being outside in the large
sparkle of stars, the air
like Seven-Up.
She wears a knitted red toque,
mitts on a string, moccasins
soaked with the smoke of Ojibway.

Later the father will sit at the kitchen table
and write in his journal:
Jan 5th - 32 below.
Bought 5 cords of jackpine.
On Lake of the Woods a car
has gone through the ice—
family trapped inside.

The child has not yet learned
to be afraid of winter. In her cellar
there are potatoes and wood.
Upstairs, a mother and father.
Shouting, pulling her sled, she
runs towards the dark.

BOILED CARROTS

Sushi, tortilla, souvlaki—these words
would all have been Greek to my mother.
She dealt in white Anglo Saxon soul food:
beef and boiled carrots. As a bride
she'd been proud to master hash
and tapioca pudding.

Her spices ranged from salt
              all the way to pepper.
For excitement she looked to the onion—
used it for smothering liver.
Of course she had cloves
to stab into ham butts.

Linguini, tabouli, tofu—
who ever heard of such things?
The village my mother cooked in
wasn't global. Dryden to the east
Beausejour to the west—
these were her boundaries.

Bigotry was as common
as barley soup and slopped over
into the cookery. The Ukranians
ate something rank called garlic.
No self-respecting Canadian woman
would have that in her kitchen, although

my mother once unknowingly ate some.
In Winnipeg, her worldly big-city sister
served her salad, the pungent bulb
crushed in the bowl.

In the train coming home, my mother
twitched her nose, looked sideways,
trying to locate the foreigner.

BLUEBERRY COUNTRY

Bears might show up, my father says
and I can't tell if he's fooling. I squint
into a thousand thousand miles
of Northern Ontario jackpine,
home to Windigo, eater of children.
This morning, he has left a warning:
A stump has been turned into Bear.

Dark shaggy beast,
snout raised to the sky,
it stands as tall as a man.
I concentrate, give it Dick Tracy's Evil Eye,
turn Bear back into stump.

Over here, Mamma calls.
Handfuls of berries. Big as nickels.
Tomorrow the kitchen will float
in foaming blue pots and in December,
frost thick as fur on the windows,
we'll eat stewed berries,
biting on bits of bush twigs,
tasting summer
when my jam tin held barely one layer
and I'd spilled the can twice and
my sister maneuvered to tip
these lean pickings from my hand.

We'd been fighting all morning;
in between fights, we swapped jokes
but the truth is she hated me.

Knock knock who's there? Windigo?
Here take my sister.

HOLIDAY AT GRANDMA'S

Wrapped in layers of musty shawls,
an organdy cap on her scant white hair,
my grandmother,
deaf, half blind,
all day in her rocker.

Uncle arranges her chair
near the pot-bellied stove in the parlour.
Brings tea. *Are you warm enough, Ma?*
He is her youngest, never married.
He cooks and keeps a bachelor's house—
old newspapers, the floor never washed.
But a good man,
the neighbors say; they don't know

about his hands, how they hunger
on hot afternoons when Mamma naps upstairs,
how they come at me, large sticky-legged beetles
clambering, voracious for tender fruit.

Grandma sleeps, or seems to sleep.
Her glasses slip down her nose,
her whiskery chin
rests on the ragbag of her chest.
Beneath her shawls, around her chair

an ancient web of silence
spreads through the drowsy house, upstairs
and down, smothers ears, clogs mouths,
catches me on Uncle's knee.

THE NEIGHBOUR'S SON

Sly tormentor; two paths of constant snot
running down like larvae.
I tangled with him once
only. He snatched my licorice whip.
I kicked; he laughed,
caught my foot
held it
for as long as it took.

When I think of him now, I think
of the way I danced for him:

a one-legged doll.

SKINNY BIRD

I was her delicate child;
too pale, she clucked, too small.
I hung around the kitchen table,
watched her flute and carve
hen tracks in the pastry
or feed the mincer's twisted throat
scraps of Sunday roast.
Into my mouth she popped
prize pickings: a salted radish,
a slice of sugared apple.

One day she fed me bone marrow;
scooped the jelly
from the yellow ring,
heaped it on a soda biscuit.
Try, she coaxed, *my skinny bird.*
I rolled it over on my tongue,
found it sweet,
asked for more, more.
Would not let her be
until she'd emptied out the bone.

HEAVEN AND HELL

Just think, twice a week, as a child,
for the sake of my clitoris,
I risked the devil
twisting me on his tine
like a hapless wiener.
Holding me over the flames
till I bubbled.

Clitoris, I've got to hand it to you.
Tucked away in your floppy quilts
you were small, uneducated, virtually
penniless, not traditionally pretty,
but you held in your tiny top knot
more power than Christ or the Pope.

Little Kleite, in you the universe
had encoded its love song.
One twang of your bliss
and I was yours, easily
forsaking the saints
in their bleak Christian heaven.

OUR LADY

My heart leapt with the heart
of the woman in a hovel,
a baby trapped in her bones,
who saw tears fall like diamonds
from the paper eyes of Our Lady's
picture pinned over her bed.

At church where red candles
shadowed her naked feet,
I watched for a quiver of lid,
a liquid gleam in the blue painted iris.
I knew she could slip inside plaster,
shake frozen folds loose,
make locked eyes flutter and smile.
At any moment a rose
might unfold, fall
       from her alabaster palm.

But My Madonna, My Queen
of Angels, of Heaven, played favourites.
She liked girls whose knees
bled on stone floors
when they scrubbed for their mothers,
little saints who never fought with their sisters,
never played with their petals.

In her nook, week after week,
still as death, she stared past me
at the same eternal spot.

MY FATHER TEACHES ME ABOUT MEN

From my bedroom window
a sweep of scrub bush and Kenora rock
and looming tall
against the northern sky
the Ontario Minnesota Pulp and Paper Mill.

I never pulled down the blind.
Who out there in the dark could see me?
Only chipmunks or the neighbour's calico cat.
Not even deer, certainly not bear.
(In those days, wild animals
didn't have to live in town.)

But who can see me? I asked
when my father said: *Close your blinds!*
The men at the Mill, he replied.
They stand out on the metal walkway
high on that middle building
where the wood is smashed to pulp.
They can see you.

I peered from my window.
       I couldn't see them.
They were too far away.
I thought of them
lounging against the distant rail
sucking a smoke
rolled from Bull Durham—

strange men with powerful eyes
that could rake the dark,
devour at leisure.

THE BATH

(For my brother, an alcoholic, who
at the age of 27, drowned in a pool)

The girl watches her mother
set out the basin,
dip her elbow, testing the water
for the new baby's bath.

Mother, I had a strange dream.
I saw white hands floating like soap.

Wind rattles the windows
but the kitchen is warm;
the wood stove has a stomachful
of crackling pine and on the oven door
the mother heats a clean towel.
Something to wrap him in.

All that night, he lay alone on the bottom.

The baby sprawls on his mother's lap
displaying his watered-silk skin
and, below the pot belly,
                        his bud like a rose.

Mother, I saw white hands
floating like lilies

The mother murmurs.
The little girl hovers; she can't stop
beaming, she's in love. She laughs
at the funny bent legs drawn up
like a Sunday roast chicken's,
tries to capture the fluttering feet,
hold them: Two soft velvet mice.

Breasts & Bellies

Day and Night are in love
Each has caught the other's foot
and they go around.

ꜟ Rumi

SOMEWHERE A GOD LAUGHS

Somewhere a god holds in his mind
an image of lovers
astride the horse of their bliss
riding and dying

Careless, they leap through
loose floating clouds of eggs
and tadpoles who watch their chance
to snatch parents
slide in between, find their way
to that warm spandex muscle
grow little hands
hang on for dear life

Somewhere a god holds
an image of lovers
knows as long as he holds it
lovers keep leaping
babies keep coming
and he laughs, slapping his thighs
amazed at his own ingenuity

FEELING FINE, SAVING MONEY

When I was fifteen, I didn't wear panties.
Why waste hard-earned money on silk or lace
no one could see?

Exposure never entered my mind.
Too dumb. I swung along
my cool little ass
bouncing loose, bare as an apple.

Only the breeze knew my secret.
It tickled its way
up my skirt, sipped
honeysuckle rose, stirred
little curls, sighed.

WITHOUT WARNING, MY MOTHER

One day, without warning, my mother
lay down with the earthworms

left all she had known
for earthworms
all her children
left standing
hand in hand
in small dresses
and trousers
with tears
on their cheeks
and Father
she left
broken-hearted

Mamma
what were you thinking?
What voice did you answer
that called you away
to the world
underground
where earthworms
toil to make earth
from the hands
and feet
the faces
of mothers?

BREASTS AND BELLIES

In those days
my breasts and belly
like a field perhaps
ploughed by the moon
I was nature's favorite
I teemed with cycles
waxed and waned
swarmed with life
cast off the egg
held the egg
birth raged through me
I arched   heaved   panted
I screamed beautifully
my body was a river
down which the blind babies
turned and twisted
lost their way
found it again

it seemed my belly
was always tender
or cramped
my nipples
tough and brown
I was swollen or stretched
or bloody or torn oh it was
splendid

AT TWENTY-TWO I TWO-STEPPED INTO MARRIAGE

At thirteen, I learned to follow.
What a thrill when my toes caught on,
latched on to his,
let themselves follow! Follow! Follow!
A rag doll, I swayed in his arms.
My knees, brushing his, picked up signals
kept me on course. His course.

Soon
there wasn't a man
                I couldn't follow.
If he danced like a bird, I flew.
If he was a buffalo
moving through mud, I was a cow
plodding beside him. I could be

anything he wanted.

MOTHERS

They'll announce:
      I've had enough!
I'm letting him go!

But when the child struggles
to loosen her hands
he finds himself in the grip
of two miniature pitbulls
Oh wait, she'll say

and when he runs to the gate
she'll follow, shameless—
you've forgotten your sweater
she'll call, your clean sox
why don't you stay
I'll cook you kraft dinner

She was finished that woman
the day he staked out her womb
clung like a limpet
began padding his shadowy bones
with her blood. She remembers
(mothers are always remembering)
when he was a baby—
how he screamed, eyes wild
the minute she left the room
Ah, she was his true love, his only

Now he wants
to go far away
He might phone, but
only for money
she'll try to hold him
the way she tried
(as a child) to hold the wild cat
they found in the barn

before it's over
(it'll never be over)
there'll be blood and howling

MENINGITIS

for Emma

That morning, death showed up
in the yard, dazzling the boy

who ran into his mother, crying:
The snow hurts my eyes.

And she at the stove
stirring

his favorite soup for lunch,
blind to the feast

that was well underway
in his small tender spine,

frowned, put down her spoon,
laid her hand on his forehead

ablaze with a fire
her fierce love

would be
unable to quench.

DRUMMING UP THE DEAD

Late at night, the rain drums the dead
from their graves. On huge slow feet
trailing clumps of earth,
they enter my house, circle, shift,
start their old stories.

Aunts jostle, plucking my sleeve.
Listen, they say,
let me tell you my side of things.

But where is my mother?

Mamma, I call, are you here tonight?

Mamma. It's her first and last name.
When she hears it she always responds,
this woman who lives in a kitchen,
potatoes counting her days.
I can not separate her from the walls
or the linoleum, or the thick plates
in the cupboard. She is morning and evening;
geraniums, scissors and pie crust.

Now I am old, and some days,
irrational as a child,
I want her back, back in her kitchen,
rattling her pots of carrots and turnips,
sloshing the blue rinse and Oxydol.
I want to come home from school,
throw my tam on a chair, say:
Mamma, I'm glad you're here,
you've been gone a long time.

The wind rises, the dead shuffle,
it's time to leave. The drumming
is deafening.

WATER

If I were to throw myself
on the ground
it would bruise me, it would
try to break my arms, but water
you move aside
make room for me, inside you

I recognize
a playful divinity—
I hear laughter, inside you

there is nothing to impede me
there is only
your boneless body
full of openings. I bring you
my bones and at once

with your wide open mouth
you rush
to explore me. Water

when you rock me
I almost remember
a grotto of waters
where I tumbled, small
sleek as an otter. There

my ear buds unfolded
the first song poured in
and you were the singer.

SUDDEN DEATH

After the mother's death
a great waiting went on
the kettle in the kitchen

waited day after day
and the table and straight-backed chairs
waited with the patience of wood

on the sill small pots of geraniums
waited silently in rows
tiny green and red children

frightened for their lives
the back door waited and the latch
alert for her hand

the front door
took on an air of expectation
while upstairs in her bedroom

week after week
a nightgown waited
long and white on its closet hook

RAPTURE POURED IN WHERE MY MOTHER HAD BEEN

My mother, one evening
stepped out
of her body, left it
like a bag of laundry
on the floor
of the Community Hall.

The minute she was out
she wanted back in.
Too much space
nothing to cling to.

She wasn't good at departures.
It took her days to prepare
a two hour train trip to Winnipeg.

She thought of her kitchen:
supper dishes piled in the sink
the disgrace. And in her bedroom
clothes flung on the bed
powder spilled
on the shiny dark dresser
traces of unconfessed sins.

She looked down at her body
saw its sprawl, its finality,
saw the circle of friends
shoulders half turned
wanting to run
from this hugeness
she had imposed on their lives.

Her last thought arrived:
*my children…who will look after…*then
like flimsy houses in a flood
dishes, children and sins
were all swept away—
and

THE MIDWIFE

Verily, except ye be born again
ye shall not enter the Kingdom of God

There is blood on her sleeves;
surgical scissors
wink at her waist.
With her large scrubbed hands
she is waiting to catch me
when I slip from the wetness of sin.
One hard clip will shear
the tough muscled cord
dangling from the cells in my brain
where desire throws tantrums.

If the birth turns nasty,
she has other tools.
She'll try anything: broken bottles,
grappling irons, two-bitted axes.
She is there to deliver me.

Harder! she hisses as I pass.
Push harder!

TRUE LOVE

There are lions on the loose;
they roam where they please.
A woman saw one in a park;
it stepped from the shrubs, huge-headed.
Before she could stop herself
she entered the bush
threw herself at his feet.

He was beautiful,
a golden-maned king from the bestiary.
With his rough skillful tongue,
he licked her face and neck.
She was wild for him.
The gods entered her blood,
she rolled over and over,
in her throat a strange mewling.

To please him she ran in the hunt,
spraddled the flesh
of shivering bodies,
rode out the death throes.
After the kill, they lounged in the sun,
cleaned blood from their nails and teeth.

When he asked her
to stalk and bring home
young women
she complied.

MARILYN MONROE AT THE MORGUE

Here on the cold slab
the Goddess of Centerfolds,
Aphrodite, flat on her back.

Look—the world renowned breasts!
Under harsh lights, they are only
the breasts of a dead woman.
The vagina that entertained
the phalli of a President
and three foster fathers
has been stuffed with hospital cotton.

And that famous face!
Wherever she is now,
she has taken her beauty with her,
left behind grey exhaustion.
The mouth, fallen open, looks famished.
Fed valium and champagne,
it begged for bread.

A camera clicks, the last picture is taken:
Smile Marilyn, show us more cleavage.
Is it true about Bobby?
Somebody fix her hair for chrissake,
it's a mess.

A passing attendant squeezes a nipple.
Hey, Marilyn! Behind their masks
the gowned doctors laugh.

THE TOLSTOYS

Leo's God hated hard cocks and
soft creamy cunts, ah poor Sonya,
poor Sonya, the gift that she was—
never fully tasted.
Leo, disgusted, dipping into
this hot and sweet curry,
this crème brulee, this divine manifestation,
with his ruined Christian soul.

After a while Sonya, sane, healthy Sonya,
began to go crazy.
All she wanted was Leo to fuck her with all his heart.
Her handsome Leo, her storyteller,
with his brooding grey eyes.

All she wanted was Leo
to stop raving about Christ,
come to rest
in his lovely strong body, in her luscious body,
enfold her, put his penis inside her.
And the two of them, the two of them together,
murmuring and laughing,
find Jesus and God and the angels
singing and plucking
their harps right there
in their bed.

THE COOKIE CUTTER

By day he was a cookie cutter;
Twenty dozen cookies cut
And counted every hour.
After eight, in small cafes
He sipped lattes, shyly
Showed a muscle to the ladies.

The ladies smelled the sugar
On his skin, sidled up,
Tripped their hips,
And with their lady-slipper tongues
Hooked the crystal grains of sugar
Caught inside his cutter's collar.

He loved the way the ladies'
Lazy wrists flicked like fish
Amongst the pink biscotti, loved
The way their shoulders slid
Into the slippery glossy slopes
Of arms, loved the belly swell
Inside their satin panties where
It flowed into the dells
And bushy dingles. And oh

He loved the winks
Their lashes sprinkled when
He nibbled at the milk ducts
Of their nipples.

In the mornings cookies curled
In kinky circles from his cutter.
Sometimes he poked the dimpled dough
And lightly slapped; sometimes
He bent and bit, waiting
All the while for dusk
When the small cafes
Set up their tables,
And the ladies
Painted on their faces,
And the flirting hour began.

PASSING JUPITER

We woke in the night
to make love
seals slipping into the sea

the universe
floated in through our window, stirring
the curtains, arranging planets

and moons on the ceiling
In the blue velvet spaces
between worlds, I asked

do you know we are just passing Jupiter?
Yes, he said. (He comes along
on these trips, who knows how)

and he named the galaxies
I carry in my body—
with his hands he named each one

that night when the universe
came in through my window
I understood the unsayable

REGINA VAGINA

These are the generations
the women of miracles
who gave birth without vaginas
beginning with Mary, ever Virgin
whose body beneath blue folds
was hairless and dry as plaster
without entrance or exit
without the dark cave
        surrounded by bush
where the cuntalini lies coiled

right up to and including
Elizabeth R, a long line of tricksters
achieved this wonder
tabula rasa between the legs

O obliterated vagina
O unknown, untasted word
O poor lonely body part
today
        let's talk about you
let us look closely
gaze into your wild glistening eye
take your picture
for the *Times*: Vagina Honoured
Cuntry admits they exist
admits God made them
admits Jesus knew about them

Vagina Most Holy every day
let me put my hand down
to say hello, I love you, dear orchid face
dear squishy scintillating slit
dear lickety lickety split
dear buried treasure
folded into your soft cloth of rose
let me remember each morning
to praise you Vagina, O Regina Vagina
seated so snugly
on your throne of thighs
O thou curly headed queen
O thou honeysuckle rose
O smart cookie

And thou, dear clitoris
I myself deeply regret
not bringing you forth
all those years in the closet
I might have mentioned you
to my member of parliament
to the mayor and council
introduced you at parties
called out your name
at matins or vespers

I might have encouraged you
to sing that song
you know by heart
the one that maketh me
praise creation, that sendeth me
galloping on the horn of plenty
that spinneth me off the wheel

THE POPE DREAMS ABOUT WOMEN

Thousands of them live in the forest.
Quick and clever, they peer
through the foliage, run
            from tree to tree.
Their scent is everywhere.
It licks at his clothes, slips past
the long hairs in his nostrils.

He is dressed in battle fatigues;
his skull cap is dappled green.
Sweating, tense, he hunts them down.

He glimpses a naked breast,
swollen with milk.
So tender, so gentle,
it terrifies him.

To his troops, he shouts orders:
Burn the forest!
Raze it to the ground!

Then he sees her. The Virgin.
She is standing on the top of a tree.
Her clothes are on fire. Flames leap
from her forehead. In her hands,
a chalice; it brims, spills over
with women's blood.
Through the roar,
            her voice rises:

Drink, she says. Drink, my son.
And be whole!

SHE NO LONGER GOES TO CHURCH

She thinks of the priest
Standing, gowned, on his altar,
His penis and brown wrinkled sac
Snug as a sniper's nest
Under his skirt.

She thinks of her husband
Erect in his pew,
His face as smug
As the priest's
Both fashioned in the image of God.

When he comes home
He will carry the smell
In his cuffs of pulpits
Dust and snuffed candles.

In her room, she disrobes
Leans close to the mirror
Touches each breast, her vulva.

In The Name of The Mother
She whispers, And of The Daughter
And of The Holy Grail.

QUOTING POPEYE

My father disliked the French priest
who inflicted long sermons
en francais to a parish
of Irish and Ukrainian Catholics
with perhaps a Pole
or two in the pews.

He liked to tell
how he caught the French priest
eating bacon on toast
at the Queens on a Friday
when everyone else had to eat
finnan haddie or beans without pork.
He lost all respect; it was as good
an excuse as any for leaving the church.

He never went back—except once.
After my mother died. Broken-hearted
he would have tried anything.

When he walked in, my brother,
an upstanding member
of the Knights of Columbus, wept.
Ten years of novenas
and fervent consultations
with the French priest
had finally paid off.

Not so. My father found the church
as devoid of life
as the pig butchered
for the priest's sinful sandwich.

When his time came to die,
he refused holy oils. Traveling light
he stood before God and declared:
I am what I am. And that's what I am.

HOW THE POPE LIKES HIS WOMEN

He likes them in kitchens
stuffing sausage.
Litters of children snuffling.

You can bet he likes them
in convents, trapped faces
in veils, pale bodies
smothered in black
damp as mushrooms.

He adores obedient women
brain pans scrubbed clean
not one impure thought
left to smolder.

He loves them drowned
in shame, down on their knees
praying to Mary and Jesus
to help them control
their cunning kleitoria.

On his altars he likes them
clutching a duster
replenishing
torn bread,
decanters of blood.

GOD FLEES THE PALACE

If you meet the Buddha on the path, kill him.

God is everywhere, Sister said,
her brain pinned so tight inside her wimple
it had fallen asleep and failed
to recognize the truth
her tongue had spoken.

Instead she pictured a powerful Man,
everywhere at once, watching the world,
watching me being lazy, being mean,
saying *damn*, saying *bugger*.

Later, on the path, I met the Buddha;
I let him live and when he sort of smiled,
Sister's god packed up his phallus,
fled the palace and

a new god rose up
vast and wild,
galaxies for hair,
black holes for eyes,
a thread from Sister's wimple
dribbling from its boundless mouth.

BLOOD FATHERS

I know one of your secrets, mighty Lion.

You show up when the lioness is away
hunting food for her family.
Your huge head, a gigantic sunflower,
fills the door of the den.
It transfixes the cubs. The boldest one
steps forward, feints, dances,
bats at the petals.

You eat him first.
Next, his brother.
Now their flesh
is back in your loins
where it began.

Later you spread your stuffed body
under a tree. Sleepy-eyed father.
The rough towel of your tongue
leisurely cleans the crevices of your paws,
nibbles, licks them clean
of the blood and scum of your sons.

HOW DOES ONE DRESS IN HEAVEN

Does Jesus walk around in a loincloth
his burning inside-out heart
pinned like a jewel to his ribs?

And Mary—does she stand barefoot
her heel on a snake and day after day
does she wear that blue thing, does she
ever want to go shopping
       try on a red thing? And the angels

how do they put on those nightgowns?
Are there wing holes, first
one wing, then a great flapping
and twisting to shove in the other? What a struggle
to face every morning of eternity. Do they
ever want to give up, say
Mary lend me your blue thing?

Eve, does she skulk outside the gate
still clutching a leaf to her privates,
eternal cock teaser, slut for all seasons,
the leaf growing old, curled at the edges,
allowing a glimpse
of something
     dark
        and beautiful.

How will I dress in heaven?
Shall I put on a neutrino
all the mornings of forever?
Or the petals that drift
from the bodies of saints?

To pass the timeless, shall I
seek out Saint Paul? He'll be wearing
a suit and a buttoned-up hair shirt.
In my Zen bra and my panties of gold
I'll stalk him
down the halls of eternity,
never ceasing to express my opinions,
setting him straight, night and day.

THE FIRST ELEPHANT

For Lorraine

It took her millennia
to create
all those wrinkles
her fingers
fatigued with crimping

when she started
the ears
she never dreamed
they would fly
from the head
like tents in a wind

and the nose
she couldn't stop
pulling the clay
out further and further
oh what is this crazy thing
I am making she said
I love it

shaping the feet
she laughed
these are the biggest
damn feet
colossal! It must be

an elephant
she called to the people
look! A mountain
has stepped
down from the sky

it walks on the plain
now find me a spirit
to match

find me
elephant spirit

THE RETURN OF THE MAMMOTH

In Siberia, thirty thousand years ago,
an infant twelve feet long
lay down its massive baby head,
stretched out its chunky legs
and died.

Today, a young scientist, ambitious
to be first at anything, squats
beside the frozen mammoth
scraping DNA.

To the camera he confides
his colossal dream: He wants to
slip the DNA
into an elephant egg,
turn time helter skelter,
drag the woolly past, alive and snorting,
into the present
before the future has arrived—

Has he asked himself: Is there room?
Do we need resurrected bodies,
humped and shaggy,
dropping turds as big as truck tires,
eating thirty thousand leaves an hour,
nudging, looking for a place
amongst the scheme of things?

In laboratories, new gods
are editing an ancient script
when all they know is science fiction.

Not a tale to live by, not a tale
for a cold winter's night.

ONCE THERE WERE TIGERS

In a forest in India the tigers
are being harvested
as if they were pig weed.

A poacher takes aim
the bullet enters the brain
and the fire god falls.

On the ground where it lies
no seeds disperse.
No new tiger grows, no flame
leaps from this dust.

How many thousands of nights
the goddess dreamed
before the face of the tiger appeared.
She rose from her bed, breathed beauty
huuuuuuaa   huuuuuuuaa
it poured from her mouth
and a head loomed out of the mist.
When she saw what she'd made,
she couldn't stop shouting: *Come look!*
The tiger is here!

PLANET EARTH

When She first saw its face
How She smiled. A daughter! She said.
Let Earth be your name.
And she ran her hand
Across blue crumpled skin,
Wetted Her fingers to slick back
The rough tops of trees,
Wild tufts of grass.

This child, She said, ah, this child
Is special. And She called
To the world of dreams for Godmothers
To come running with baskets
Spilling gifts. Birds!
Cried one, tossing feathers and beaks.
Fish! said another, throwing scales
And fins. Animals! shouted the third,
Juggling fur, hooves and snouts.

And people, said a voice
From the shifting shadows
Where the devil, grinning, slouched.

People.

BACK ON THE LONGING TRAIN

Longing arises out of that aspect of the mind
that is pulling the mind back to its source

Ganga-ji

I've only had one real lover
and the bugger is in hiding
somewhere in the Rockies or the rainforests
or behind a cactus in the Gobi desert.

Heartless! Why did you send me out
on this damned safari?

Weren't we happy together?

Or was it I who left?
Was I ever that hare-brained?

Do you miss me?

This ad in the paper—

Divine Being, old, lonely, n/s,
s/d, likes astronomy

Is that you?

STIGMATA

In grade three we heard rumours.
Something ahead for us.
Huge. Formless. Had to do with blood.

Slowly, the intelligence filtered down.
Betty's sister who was ten,
who was old, told Eileen
who told Marie and me,
  (our mouths falling open)
that every month
  (the spectre taking shape)
our sides would rip open
and blood would pour out.

Middle-aged
I can still feel the wound—
here—
just under my ribs.

THE MORNING HOLDS ME IN ITS ARMS

It swarms me softly as I walk
comes with me into the forest
where the fallen fir is telling its story—
the beginning, the middle and the end—
one long sentence, every word of it true.

Everywhere, this story—in the scatter
of orange feathers and small intestines
on the grass, dissolving into
the kindness that is earth.
My body dissolving in love in the night
is caught in the plot. The morning itself
is dying in the arms of noon.

In Haida Gwai,
fallen totems kiss the earth,
surrender their faces and tongues.

The earth wants us back.
Standing still in the forest
I hear it calling—
the very dirt reaches up.

When I listen to its voice
I want to lie down
with the fallen trees.

GOD IS EVERYTHING

For Ramana Maharshi

1.

Of course he's in the mountain, the rose
but is he in the blowfly
the cat shit; is he in
my bathing suit
      dripping from the rack
            displaying its inside-out
                  beige foam breasts—

those foam breasts, are they god?

2.

What sort of vast sprawling pop art,
what clumsy collage is this god?
Bathing suits and breasts
a planetful of trees, trucks and television sets

3.

and eyes—
      your luminous eyes—

Ramana

what wide-awake god
      is this looking out?

KUBLER-ROSS AND THE CRANEFLY

On the slab of my bathroom counter,
a cranefly lies on her back. She is raging;
her skinny legs saw the air as if
she believes she might
fly away from her death.
Playing god, I set her upright.
There! Perhaps she wont die after all.

A slight trembling, the pepper-speck eyes
stare from their stalks on the bead-like head.
I barely have time to wonder
if she's grateful
when her spindly body is rocked by shudders
and a small spirit, the size of an eyelash,
pulls away, rises and is gone
leaving that terrible stillness
that goes on and on
the way the soldier keeps lying in the ditch
where he fell or my mother in her coffin
never turned her head or uncrossed her hands.
Those submissive hands. Their last pose
taken into darkness.

My mother named the cranefly: *mosquitohawk.*
Good things to have around, she said, they eat mosquitoes.
I never caught one with a mosquito leg dangling
from its jaws; did she lie to me? The little body
of the cranefly too is obedient in death.
Her flawless wings are neatly aligned, her knees,
the size of crumbs, intersect her delicate legs.
What a strange waste of beauty and design, those wings.
The disregard of the rich.

In my bathroom I find myself
unthinkingly moving through Kubler-Ross's stages,
miniscule but complete.
Here is the need to comfort the dying,
the interference (to comfort myself),
the ridiculous flair of hope,
the cold curiosity, the puzzle of endings.
After death the sadness, merely a teaspoon
but the same flavour as a cupful.

And the decision: What to do with the body?
I can't leave it there—the death lesson
every time I open the bathroom door.
I always abandon the Buddhist when
he heads for the charnel grounds
to sit with the corpses. I especially can't bear
to watch slow disappearance. After all,
there are people I love, there is
my own absurd life to live.
After two days, I carry the body outside
lay it softly among the geraniums.
So many deaths, common as rain.
On window sills, in gardens, in train wrecks.
Each
should be attended,
and grieved,
or else none.

POST MODERN FUNERALS

Where's the body, I ask, the dead body . . .

What strange times we live in
when a body can't attend
its own funeral.

In church, the live bodies stand, sit, kneel.
At the altar the priest mutters,
pretends he has hold of the body
of Christ. Now there are two absent bodies.

A funeral needs a coffin with an occupant.
A place for the mind to alight.
What's it like, inside, the lid
an inch from your nose? There in the dark,

he's wearing his good suit. Shoes?
Someone has forced his fingers
around a black rosary,
his obsequious letter of passage.

There is barely room for his elbows.

Once we laid out our dead in parlours.
There they were, right in our way.
For three days, the family
looked and looked. Nothing happened.

Then they knew.

Old Woman

In the whole of the universe, there are only two—
The Lover and the Beloved.

* Irina Tweedie

LOOSE WOMAN

Old Woman has let go of her sadness now;
she has shed her allotment of tears.
She has broken her sugar bowl, spilled her sugar
into the dust bin, collected her coins.
Is she angry?

Yes, she is angry.

She no longer sits at her place
by the chimney. Where has she gone?
She is roaming the halls—this way
and that. Her hair is loose. Her tongue.
She shouts questions,
rattling on doorknobs. In the rooms

the directors hear her pass; the long table
shudders, cracks split the wood.
Her feet have grown large, they say.

Their eyes slide sideways; they adjust
their ties; their hands grip their testicles.
She is loose! they whisper.
We must burn her again.

There is no fire
hot enough, no rope strong enough.
The serpent leaps from the ground
to encircle her arm. She gathers
the winds at her back. Even now
the trees in the night whisper
and plot to assist her.

The spirits of minerals rush to her side.
She holds council with the tribes underground,
with the clay and the roots and the caves.

Nothing can stop her.

She is loose!

OLD WOMAN SPEAKS

Old Woman says for her birthday this year
she doesn't want a china cup
or a tea cozy or another
antimacassar for her sofa.

Nor does she want a nice picture
of Jesus weeping in the garden.

What she wants this year
is a man
with an erection as hard
and long as the leg
of her kitchen table.

CODEINE AND ROSES

For Mae Hill Brown

We split a ginger ale
the old poet and I.
Here's to you friend.
Our conversation unfolds,
old fabric, stroked
and ironed out with words.

We talk about husbands—she recalls
the day of her wedding.
September, nineteen thirty-two.
The winds of the Great Depression
whistled through everyone's coat.

For the party, her mother
somehow managed a miracle:
Chicken à la king, elegantly
served in shells for her daughter.
All the neighbours were invited.

She remembers her father. Anxious
and clumsy with love, he put his foot
through her veil, ripped the muslin.

Sixty-five years have gone by.
Her mother, her father with his foot,
the long-ago neighbours
are all bones in the graveyard.

She sighs. All week she has struggled
with pain. At night it is *exquisite*,
she says. Codeine doesn't touch it.
But, she confides, just before dawn
the petals of that rose
on the table were unfolding
and they whispered to me:

Joy, joy.

THE SECRET

Hours
  crouched
    with the intensity
     of a lover
 trying to catch,
        to cup and caress,

a sparrow—
  a small chirping sparrow
    hopping just out of reach.
     There's a secret, my mother whispered:
      put salt on its tail.

Salt in my pocket
  I stalked. I never caught
    one single bird.

But that didn't matter. I knew
  the secret
    for catching birds.

When the time came to leave home,
  I went out alone, but sure
    that somewhere,
     there was someone
      who would whisper

the secret
  for catching the bird
    who sits high on the mountain
     crying: *Freedom!*

And I looked
  and I looked
    and I'm old, I'm old

and I'm looking

TRYST

An old woman wakes in the night
to find a child by her bed
dressed for first communion:
white dress, white shoes,
a bridal wreath pinned to her hair.

Startled the old woman cries out:
Who are you? Although she knows
this small bride of Christ
is herself as a child of six,
the mask of old age peeled away.

She feels on her wrist
a soft touch. *Is it time?*
The child smiles and far back
in her guileless eyes
a wise old woman looks out.

Yes, the child nods,
and we must hurry,
the bridegroom paces.

OLD WOMAN OFFERS A SERMON FOR DAUGHTERS

There is one thing you've got to understand about men.
Old woman leans back in her rocker,
adjusts her wrinkles,
addresses her daughters.

Men, Old Woman says—bending to stroke
the head of the elegant wolfhound bitch
who eternally lies at her feet—
men never doubt they are ruled
by the cool god of reason. Truth is

their minds seldom stray from that
long-nosed monkey
below the Trunk at the Junction.
This monkey never stops howling
for reassurance and extravagant praise.
Yea, even adoration.

Daughters, Precious Ones
Old Woman pauses—
her vast belly wobbles and ripples,
cosmic laughter rocks the room—
Daughters, Precious Ones,
(she slaps her broad knee)
that's the first

and the last thing
to understand about men.

A YOUNG HUSBAND

At dusk, the old woman
likes to sit by herself
listening
to the footfalls of the dead.

Behind a thin curtain of air,
wearing slippers of satin
they practice
walking meditation.
Lift and place, lift and place.

She remembers
a young husband, the first time
he dressed in front of her.
He put on a white shirt, his arms
folding and lifting like wings,
his obsidian head like a god's.
How stunning his darkness
against the white cotton.
His beauty always
        softened her belly.

Listening
she separates his footstep
from the others,
hears it draw closer,
laughs to herself
when she sees
a silk-slippered toe
lift the hem of the curtain.

HOUND AND OLD WOMAN GIVE WARNING

Old Woman is back. She's stirring her pots.
What's in the pots? Trouble. Big trouble.
Crouched beside her, an odd looking streak.
What is it? It's Hound. Long bony head
like a skull picked clean, paws big as drums.
Hound and Old Woman—traveling companions
since before the Big Bang. They know
certain things: Out there. Inside. Underneath.

Hound sniffs the air, he loves trouble,
his yellow eyes glint with splinters of trickery.
He howls when Old Woman throws into the pot
a handful of pepper from hell
a few grains of snuff, two teeth from a mud shark.
Old Woman, he says, when the communion food is ready,
let's look up a T.V. evangelist, that one
who thinks God is a Christian man
in a suit and tie, someone you slap on the back.
Let's spin him through a quasar, put quarks on his tongue,
teach him the ancient cryptogram:
God is dog spelled backwards. Yeah, God is

a giant Rotweiler escaped from his kennel, roaming loose.
Old Woman laughs, slaps her spoon on the kettle,
throws in a cup of black holes, some bear's blood.
You dog, you, you're my favourite person.
You know who you are, you know
what you're doing here. Listen
Hound of my Dreams, forget the preacher.
Load up the wagon with this bucket of trouble.
Let's go to the fields of death.
Let's go to a clearcut.

WHERE DOES THE RADIANCE GO

this tree
     at the end of my driveway
          this Lombardy Poplar

when it shakes its October arms
     shouts *Hey!*
          I cover my eyes, stagger

the woman clothed in the sun
     throwing streams of light
          I can't bear to lose

the glory
     but already little by little
          it's leaving

nothing I say or do
     will make it
          change its mind

OLD WOMAN COMES OUT OF HER CAVE AND PUTS THE WORLD IN ORDER

Old Woman shambles out of her cave,
feeling sulky, feeling troublesome.
Lifts her hand to swat the gaping moon
from the sky, flings it
like a broken egg across the stones.
Looks around for Old Man.
Love, she says. I need love.

Down by the river Old Man sits on a branch.
He has turned himself into a bluejay.
Rrrrr, he says, preening indigo feathers,
eating a wood louse, hoping to fool
Old Woman. Rrrrrr. He knows
she will wear him out, reduce
his delicate penis to flummery.

Jay, says Old Woman, have you seen Old Man?
Meow, says Jay, I mean Rrrrr, rrrrr.
Old Man has gone into the woods;
craving truffles he has taken his spade
and . . . Swat! Old Woman's hand
swings through the air.
Damn liar, she swears. You are Old Man.
Now come be my lover, be brave, show me
your prickly wild thistle
that grows in the bracken.

Old Man succumbs. Cannot resist
a chance to display his favourite thing!
His springboard of champions, his longboat,
his Cedar of Lebanon, his Eighth Wonder
whose lift and heft
has kept him in thrall since boyhood.

Now it leaps up. Beautiful purple,
eagerly gleaming, pin-eyed pet. And
once again Old Woman rolls him over
in a tumult of dust and sweet clover.
Ravages, savages, peels the stem,
snaps the blossom, transforms
his elegant Prince of Sticks
into a miserable, shriveled escargot.

Humming, Old Woman returns to her cave;
leaves Old Man mumbling praise in the dust.
At her door, she pauses. Scoops up the streaks
of splashed moon from the stones, reshapes
the gold in her great broad palms.
Imprints it with the face of Old Woman.
Pins it back in the sky.

About the Author

Mildred Tremblay was born in Kenora. Ontario in 1925. Her book of short stories, Dark Forms Gliding, was published in 1988 and received considerable critical acclaim. Her award-winning poetry has been published in literary journals and anthologies across Canada and the United States. She lives in Nanaimo, B.C.